Protecting Your Business

Insights for startups and small business - From a master entrepreneur

New, expanded second edition

Dave Berkus

Published by David Berkus DBA The Berkus Press

For corrections, company/title updates, comments, or any other inquiries, please e-mail DBerkus@berkus.com

Second Printing 2014
10 9 8 7 6 5 4 3 2

ISBN: 978-1-105-04072-6

The content within this book has been previously published within the books, BERKONOMICS, and ADVANCED BERKONOMICS. Individual insights from this book are published periodically in Dave's emails and blog, www.berkonomics.com.

Groups may order copies of the book at a group discount by contacting Dave Berkus at 626-355-5375, or at dberkus@berkus.com .

Throughout this book, the Cambria type font was used for headlines, and text was set using the Calibri font.

Contents

Contents

INTRODUCTION

This book is the fifth in a series of eight short, easy to read books that guide an entrepreneur through the stages of creation, management, growth, and ultimately sale of a small business enterprise. And this is the second edition of this book, packed with half again as much materials the first edition, published in 2011.

Each section is an insight into another facet of starting a business that is not taught in business school or available in business texts, but rather the result of over fifty years of entrepreneurial experience with my own entrepreneurial companies and serving as investor, coach, mentor and board member for over forty entrepreneurial startups over the years.

Originally published as portions of three books, BASIC BERKONOMICS, BERKONOMCS, and ADVANCED BERKONOMICS, comments from entrepreneurs and professional managers after reading those books led to suggestions that I create separate mini-books for each stage of the business, to appeal to the interests of those at that stage of development, ready to absorb and implement insights that apply directly to the current stage of their business. Make them inexpensive and available as eBooks, they suggested, so that entire teams of managers could use the book as a planning tool and discussion prompt for the team in meetings.

And so this series of Small Business Success Books was born to address an opportunity. You can pick up this book and immediately relate to the insights, issues, opportunities, and exercises in this book right at the earliest stages of creating your business. This is not a replacement for "how to" books, courses, and consultants. It is a deeper opportunity to evaluate, plan, and execute strategies for growth based upon these insights that augment and amplify the usual "how to" materials available to entrepreneurs.

In this book, I'll tell personal stories from my fifty-plus years of entrepreneurial experience. But every one of us has a story to add to this mix, one of passionate entrepreneurism, sometimes inside an existing larger corporation, sometimes alone on a kitchen table, or back room desk. And it is a sure thing that many of us will have cogent, insightful additions to this caldron, culled from their own experiences. There's a place for these in the blog, www.berkonomics.com, and I welcome any and all for others to read and learn.

Dave Berkus

Arcadia, California

P.S. This is the sixteenth publication from *The Berkus Press*. I am very fortunate to have expert help this time from some very smart friends in the business, each of whom has volunteered to contribute one or more insights for this book, directly from their personal experience of working as an entrepreneur or with entrepreneurs. Here's a special thanks to these friends, whose contributions are definitely for your benefit. Whenever one of these excellent insights appear in this book, the first time each contributor's work appears, I'll insert a very short bio for that expert right below the headline. And as always, if no attribution appears for an insight, I'm its author - and to be blamed for any and all errors in judgment and accuracy.

Protecting Your Business

There are many stories of good businesses large and small felled by failure to insure against calamities of many unforeseen types. In this phase of our analysis into the stages of a company's life cycle, we investigate the protection of the corporate asset, using commercial tools and insights that cost nothing more than knowledge, with the board and management watching for signs of impending problems both external and internal.

Contractors must really be independent!

How many of us have "hired" independent contractors over the years, a bit worried over the gray area between employee and contractor as defined by the IRS? I've experienced the results of a wrong decision, and the IRS and state agencies are not forgiving in their pursuit of penalties, interest and most damaging, assessing a company with the on both employer and employee taxes when reclassifying the person as an employee.

Yes, that's right. The company must pay the employee's portion of the taxes (and penalties on these) as well as paying those they would have paid if the person were an employee.

And the IRS has raised the bar on its test as to whether an independent contractor is not in reality an employee. So it is important – no really urgent – that we review some of the twenty – yes twenty – tests the IRS now uses to determine if a person is an independent contractor.

1. Contract for service: An independent contractor should work under a written contract with the company, defining the end result expected, time to achieve, lump sum or unit cost, ownership of intellectual property created and more.

2. Direction: The contractor directs itself, rather than being managed as an employee. And just as important, a contractor does not supervise any of the company's employees directly. This is tricky when a contracted CFO assumes a position of directing an accounting department. Usually, in acceptable cases such as this, the contracted executive comes from a recognized agency with a history of paying its own employee taxes, health insurance, and other benefits. Without this protection, a contracted executive is suspect, even if working with more than one company at a time.

3. Integration: A contractor provides services which are not an integral part of the core business of the employer. This one is tricky. Is a

contracted CFO an employee because the CFO job is integral? How about a contractor CEO? The person must pass all the other tests when one of them, such as this, crossed into the very gray zone.

4. Individual on the job: A contractor may hire a substitute without the company's permission – although the company should then be able to terminate the contract with the contractor if the substitute is not acceptable.

5. Term: A contractor is hired for a specific project, usually tied to a time term. An undefined period of time favors the ruling as employee.

6. Reporting: Here is a surprise. The IRS wants to test that a contractor is NOT required to submit regular reports. Yet, most of us would want to have such documentation of progress other than an invoice.

7. Tools and materials: The contractor must supply his or her own tools. This is tricky when a contractor sits at your desk using your computer and your phone system all day.

8. Physical facility: The contractor must have its own "home office" even if in a bedroom, from which primary work is performed.

9. Works for more than one company: If such a person works only for a single company for any period of time, that person will probably be determined to be an employee. A contractor must make services available to the general public.

10. Termination: A contractor works under a contract – which means that an independent contractor cannot be "fired," as long as results are satisfactory as defined within the contract of service.

There are more tests, but these are the ones most often used by the IRS. States add a few of their own; so beware. Pay contractors using account payable systems, not payroll services. Pay only upon receipt of invoices, not with regularly triggered checks or transfers of uniform amounts without invoice documents to back up the payments.

Many small or early stage company CEOs look for opportunities to cut cash drains, knowing that payroll is usually the greatest cash drain of all. The temptation to reduce that by fourteen percent or more by classifying a gray area employee as a contractor is very high. And that includes self-payments to a founder.

Founders working for a company are employees if they take regular payments, subscribe to company benefits, attend regular company meetings, or fail any of the tests above. The temptation to just draw cash and call it a loan, or document a year's withdrawals with a 1099 is great, but highly risky.

There is nothing worse than a large tax bill and threats of a government agency seizing a cash account when a company cannot or does not respond with proper documentation or payment. And even a single year's worth of transgressions, when added into a single tax bill with penalties and interest, can appear daunting to small and young companies.

Like payment of payroll taxes by incremental impound each pay period, as opposed to waiting until the last minute and making manual tax payments, it is a proper discipline of management to "take the hit" incrementally to protect the business from a catastrophic failure to pay a governmental agency any form of tax when and as due. Need we emphasize the personal liability of management AND the board of directors attached to tax payments?

Good management takes discipline and enough knowledge to prevent these possibly crippling errors in judgment that stem from decisions made to avoid or put off tax payments when accrued or due.

Associate with competitors. Share carefully.

Many of us belong to industry associations and find ourselves at conferences and trade shows with time to spend with competitors. Some of these are old friends; some even former associates. It is natural to want to associate with these people for many reasons, certainly socially. Most CEOs want to obtain information about their competitors in the most subtle and non-obvious ways. And of course, most are willing to trade information to get information.

In my former industry, I became an informal centralized source for knowledge about the revenues of each of the many competitors, with a special skill for asking just the right questions to obtain the information. How many employees does the firm have today? Are you profitable yet? Can you guess what percentage your revenue comes from recurring sources such as maintenance revenues? In return for the answers to these several questions, I was usually able to guess a company's gross revenues within a few percent and would state my guess to the CEO. His reaction would guide me to increase or decrease my estimate appropriately. He'd be a bit amazed with the quick fancy math work, and I would have yet another piece of the puzzle helping me to gauge the total size of the industry in annual revenues and the growth and size of competitors. All of this was immensely helpful in strategic planning and marketing, even though to this day I do not think those CEOs were aware of the value of the information so easily given. And none of this is especially considered a trade secret, violating the unspoken covenant between competitor CEOs that there is a limit to such exchanges.

On the other hand, often a sales person or marketing manager would show up at my door with a complete package of a competitor's materials, including price lists, a proposal with discount percentages clearly shown and a list of feature functionality meant to reinforce the proposal. The source of this information was typically the purchasing decision-maker for a friendly customer or candidate customer. The question is one of ethics, since the competitor certainly did not volunteer any of the information, which would have been the competitor employee's violation of confidentiality and cause for being fired. What does a CEO do with this wonderful, rich information dropped at his door at no cost or obligation? Few would destroy it and ask all to forget that it was ever in their hands. Most would absorb the information and then admonish those who had seen it to not repeat to anyone that it was in their hands. If you've been in business for long enough, you've seen your share of this gray market information. My advice is to be very careful, think of the golden rule, never use this information publicly, and certainly never reproduce it, let alone disseminate it internally.

As to sharing information to get information, CEOs and executives are bound by a duty to their corporations not to share trade secrets with anyone who has not signed a confidentiality agreement, including consultants to the company. For CEOs on the corporate board, it is a large part of the "duty of care", a legal requirement of board members to protect the assets of the corporation first and foremost, one of those assets being the trade secrets of the corporation.

The FAIRNESS doctrine.

Reduce the emotion; reduce the threat of lawsuit.

You've certainly experienced the angry outburst from an associate or employee who has just learned of an event that the person took as "unfair," no matter how rational the explanation by the decision maker.

Most emotional responses to decisions in business are generated not because the person making the response feels the decision was unwise, but rather unfair.

So I've created the "Fairness Doctrine," as a stated element in the cultural fabric of businesses where I am involved. Simply stated, a decision or action that affects an individual must be made with consideration of the affected individual's view of the fairness of that decision. This doctrine is a variant of "do unto others" but with a twist. The recipient of the decision in this case usually has little opportunity to respond in kind ("as you would have them do unto you"). It is this frustration coupled with the simple outcry of "That's not fair!" - that can affect the culture of a company in ways never considered by the original decision-maker.

People sue others and their companies usually because they feel emotionally that they have been treated unfairly, not just because they were affected financially.

Firing a person considered a key associate without any advance warnings or public revelation for the reason, such as the need to consolidate or downsize, is a good example of setting up such a groundswell of accusations of unfair treatment. Public dressing down of an employee in front of associates is inhumane and often generates a negative response from all who witness or hear of the action. Closing a highly effective department, shutting down a marginal company, canceling a promising project all are good examples of management setting up a visceral response of "unfair" among those affected.

I have often addressed the issue of maintaining the dignity of the individual in a business environment. The two are linked: the fairness doctrine and treatment of an individual with dignity, no matter how distasteful the decision implemented.

So my advice is to take the time to establish the reasons for pending actions - if not in an emergency environment. Speak privately to employees who are in danger of being fired, documenting the discussion to the employee's file. Open up to the general group with facts that might later affect them, even at the risk of losing one or more to a hunt for a new job. Most employees and associates, treated with respect and dignity, will respond with understanding and lose the emotion that might have accompanied receiving the later news of a negative event.

In fact, many times over the years, I have seen whole companies rise to new levels of efficiency, creativity, and sense of urgency when informed of the alternatives being considered by a board or management.

At the risk of losing talent not targeted, it is only fair to treat people as intelligent beings capable of understanding the dilemmas faced by management, and sometimes able to find solutions to problems not seen by those in control.

Manage your bottlenecks!

As a manager, you have a number of critical tasks that are general to your position as opposed to specific to your industry. These include ensuring the continued health of the organization, setting the moral compass for your stakeholders, providing for succession by training and documenting, leading the effort in compliance of regulations and safety needs, and ... elimination of all possible bottlenecks that impede the efficiency of your organization.

The definition of a bottleneck in your business is one that constricts the flow of work from one area to another in the flow of product or service through your organization.

A bottleneck in your organization's flow of product or service can happen, shift, or disappear quickly. Common to all bottlenecks are three factors:

1. All product, labor, and cost before the bottleneck are impeded from creating maximum efficiency by being forced to slow output or build inventories. This is a costly loss for any business and one that should be a focus for your management as soon as identified.

2. The bottleneck itself strains to keep up with demand, often to the point of reducing its own efficiency in the process of attempting to keep up with demand.
3. All processes after the bottleneck are slowed for lack of flow into their zone of control and waste time, money, space and output, always resulting in reduced revenues and profits.

You can be the bottleneck. If people are waiting for you to respond to a question or make a decision about design, process, spending for a core need, or any of tens of critical decisions, you are creating a slowing or stoppage of work before you and idle resources behind you. If this describes you at any moment in your day, you should consider removing yourself from the bottleneck list by delegation, reduction of your non-critical workflow, or (heaven forbid) increasing your hours of production.

If failing to hire a critical employee is the cause of reduced efficiency, you must act quickly to either make an effective hire or alter the environment that creates the urgent need, all to remove that bottleneck.

And if an inefficient or undersized machine or department or process is creating a backup of critical path work flow, you must address this as an urgent matter whose cost is much more than the cost of the machine or person needed, but the amplified cost of the lost output it affects.

You, as a successful manager, must be attuned to and responsible for elimination of all forms of bottlenecks within your span of control. Watch for, and stamp out, all those you identify as soon as you find them. The effect of your action is magnified several-fold at the output stage of your business, leading to increased customer satisfaction and increased profits.

Bet the farm only when the crops are on fire.

This insight addresses the amount of risk you and your company are willing and able to tolerate over time. Most people believe that early stage companies should take risks aggressively because there is less to lose and much more to gain with each risky bet or decision. Common thinking goes on to address large, public corporations by expressing that the relative tolerance to risk is decreased, in favor of protecting the brand or financial health of the enterprise.

Either way, as in a Las Vegas casino, the numbers of times risks are taken directly affect the average outcome over time. Take an extreme risk once, and you may win the bet. Your average is 100%. But for any sized company to continue to take major risks the averages will surely catch up and the rate of success falls to the mean, which we will assume to be 50% of the risks result in failure. Depending upon the size of each risk, this may be entirely acceptable, as in small bets at the gaming table.

But this insight raises the ante by addressing those risks that are game-changing, those that "bet the farm." Occasionally, a CEO must make a decision that commits all of the corporate resources to a successful outcome. Using all of the company's cash and credit to produce a new product that is untested but shows every promise of success is one such bet sometimes made by CEO's of companies large and small. Automobile companies are famous for making such bets on cars that won't be on the market for 18 to 36 months from decision date, arriving at a time when gas prices and consumer preferences may have changed dramatically during that time. Some of those bets were unbelievably successful, such as the introduction of the Ford Mustang. Some were complete failures, such as GM's emphasis upon design and production of larger cars and SUV's even as consumers were voting with dollars for smaller, fuel efficient cars from foreign manufacturers.

We must assume that the auto company CEO's made their decisions to build based upon all available information, including consumer tests and market surveys. Many smaller companies just do not have the resources to do this in depth before committing resources which loom as massive to them toward a new product. Whatever the outcome, it is a safe statement that a decision-maker should commit major resources amounting to a bet of the business only when there is little alternative, that there is so much to gain that it overcomes the crippling loss that could occur. There are only so many times a CEO can get away with succeeding with such risky strategies.

Patent litigation can kill the small guy.

When you think of patents, you think of added value to the corporation in the form of protection of its intellectual property. In fact, many corporations spend millions developing surrounding patents to form what is known as a "patent thicket," much like Brer Rabbit jumped into to protect himself against his detractors in the briar patch. Investors like to see patents or patent applications as evidence of intellectual property value and barriers to entry.

But there is a darker side to patent protection. The cost for filing patents and extending the filings to multiple countries is expensive, but often manageable. The problems come from either prosecuting or defending a patent, and those problems can come in many forms.

First, if your patent is challenged at any point, even after it has been granted, the cost of defense is dramatically higher than the original patent filing and attorney fees. It has become a common practice for large companies to fight their patent wars in the Patent Office itself, by filing legal challenges, requiring re-examination and sometimes an appeals process that can lead all the way to appeals court.

Second, if you elect to prosecute a violator of your patent, you begin a process you cannot easily abandon. Depending upon the size of the company or companies you go after, some will counter sue for violation of adjacent patents they may own, or sue for causes seemingly unrelated to the patent. This happened to one of my companies, and the cost of defense escalated out of control, exceeding the cost of prosecution, ultimately contributing to the death of the company.

Third, if you are sued in a patent case, and elect not to settle the suit early (bypassing a strategy of the prosecution), then your defense costs increase over time to reach amounts a small company CEO would never permit if in control of the situation. But to defend a lawsuit is not to control it. And patent litigation can kill the small guy.

Know and avoid Time Bankruptcy.

Time bankruptcy results from the deliberate over-commitment of core resources.

I created the term "time bankruptcy" almost thirty years ago when the computer software business was young, and I was a software developer building a young company based upon quality first. Asked to speak at a number of software industry events, I found my voice and immediate audience understanding as I described variants of the following problem to my audience. The insight became clearer as I was hired again and again to pick up the pieces of failed programming efforts by other software companies in this then young industry.

A developer would take on a new customer, customize programs as needed, and install perhaps an 80% completed system upon the customer's brand new minicomputer system. The customer would pay for all or at least 90% of the system, perhaps holding back a retainer awaiting completion. Burning through the payment and needing more to cover fixed overhead, the developer would do the same for the next 80% customer, moving on to the third. About that time, the first would call asking for completion of programming or training, firmly but politely. The fourth installation was interrupted as the first customer suggested that he would stop giving glowing recommendations for the vendor, insisting upon a completion date, while the second customer interrupted with its first call for completion. By the fifth or sixth *(who keeps count for these stories?)*, the first threatens suit, the second becomes demanding and the third makes that expected call for a completion date. So the vendor stops work on the newest installation to complete earlier installations. Revenues dry up while overhead continues to burn though the developer's pockets. It's a classic case of time bankruptcy. The developer deliberately overcommitted his prime or core resources (in this case his personal time) leading to a loss of income and reputation that it could not recover.

The same story could be constructed for any company selecting a limited number of test customers for a new product. Select too many, and pay too little attention to each. Commit all of your core resources to solving the resulting problem, and new work stops. Time bankruptcy. Not a pretty sight, and completely avoidable.

Be aware of this trap. No-one but yourself can be blamed for allowing core resources to be overcommitted, even if by subordinates. That's because you now know the term and the impact of such an error in judgment, and understand that the simple but important remedy is to slow the commitment of those most critical resources to the front lines.

Forecast your cash position to sleep more soundly.

In the past insight, we created an example to demonstrate that it truly takes money to make money; that growth calls for increases in working capital. The example we crafted proved that companies can easily find themselves strapped for cash during periods of rapid growth as well as in downturns.

There are many techniques and time horizons for forecasting cash. For those companies with constant billings to customers during a month, and for those with extra-large fixed costs such as payrolls at periods during a month, it is important to begin the discipline of the 13 week rolling forecast as a tool for finding and planning around short term cash problems. Each week, the actual cash position is updated and the past week dropped from the forecast and a new week added. This format is much more relevant to management that a monthly forecast when cash is tight, allowing for weekly planning in advance. In addition, and perhaps in place of this, for many more stable companies, a monthly cash forecast is appropriate and serves as an excellent planning tool for arranging any lines of credit or extensions of payment to suppliers over the months' time.

I've experienced periods of failure to plan short term cash needs, finding myself worrying over daily cash flow, and draining energy and focus from strategic issues. And I am sure many of you who have been in growing businesses have had this experience as well. For those of us who have lived through the worry of arranging for (or passively hoping for) cash to cover the next day's needs, this insight is a lesson learned. Even if accurate cash forecasting highlights a coming problem, the element of time and elimination of surprise both work to reduce the drain upon management, and allow for time to plan for ways to increase cash flow systematically. (See insight 65 for a few ways to do just that.)

Never use short term borrowing to cover long term debt.

This insight is one that is so important to the continued health of a growing company that it cannot be overstated. First, let's be sure we know what is short in term and what is long in term. Long term debt is taken on for the acquisition of fixed assets such as equipment, cars, facilities and acquisitions of companies or their assets. Short term debt is often composed of accounts payable to the trade or employees for expenses, payroll liabilities, accrued but unpaid vacations, customer deposits, and the portions of any loans due to be repaid within one year.

Asset-based financing is common for companies with accounts receivable and / or inventories. There are numerous lenders engaged in this practice, including most business banks. Typically, companies may arrange to borrow between 70% and 80% of those non-government receivables that have not aged past 60 days from invoice, up to a maximum amount, or "credit line". Other companies have both the creditworthiness and relative size to be able to borrow from private and banking sources without collateral, with unsecured loans. Many of these lines of credit require that the borrower "clean up the line" for one month out of every year, that is to be out of debt with the lender for that period to prove to the lender that the need for the cash is not permanent, used like a long term loan.

Numerous companies have gotten into trouble by using the easy availability of these short term lines of credit, meant for rising and falling working capital needs, to make payments upon long term obligations such as asset loan payments when due. And worse, some even purchase assets such as equipment with money from short term loans. Matching the term of a loan with the life of the asset is an important business principle. Receivables are assets for only 60 days for the purpose of these lines of credit, and the available line can be reduced automatically as receivables reduce with payments by customers or aging beyond 60 days. We all expect new receivables to be added to replace these, but a cyclic business; a disruption in the general economy; a reduction in the company's revenues would each contribute to a reduction in the amount available for such borrowing. To avoid the coffin corner of an over-borrowed asset-based line with no cash for working capital, remember that short term borrowings such as these should never be used to pay any long term obligations or to purchase fixed assets.

The value of legal advice isn't measured by a law degree.

Over the years in business and as a member of over forty boards, I have received good advice from corporate attorneys and on occasion bad advice as well. There is a line that should be drawn in a relationship between corporate attorney and CEO or board. Attorneys are paid to protect the corporation, not to give business advice. Some are experienced enough to provide great business advice. But the law degree they earned does not assure that, even though most CEO's respect the advice they receive from their attorney highly enough not to doubt the conclusions or the experience behind the conclusions offered. And since attorneys are paid to protect, often they will give a litany of warnings about what could go wrong when accepting a contract clause they have been trained to challenge. There comes a time when a CEO must decide to reject what may seem like important good advice from the attorney and chance acceptance of terms within a contract that may cause risk, but controllable risk or risk that is so remote as to be worth the acceptance of the business represented by the contract at hand.

I was chairman of a company that had been offered an investment by a Fortune 500 company making a strategic investment in our business, which was capable of driving new demand to the large company though a series of new web services creating a greater need for the large company's products. The business terms had been agreed to between the business development officer of the investing company and our board, as both companies turned the details over to their respective attorneys for documentation. The attorney for the investor was a member of a large, respected law firm in Silicon Valley, and certainly was full of himself as sole legal protector of the rights of his very significant investor. As drafts of the otherwise standard investment agreements passed from him to our attorney and our management, we immediately spotted a significant number of terms we not only had not agreed to but were contrary to the spirit of the investment. The attorney held fast at every challenge, stating that "these terms are standard for our client and cannot be changed." We appealed to the business development executive, who deferred to the attorney restating that the terms were unchangeable as far as the big company was concerned. After conferring between our attorney and board, we walked away from what would have been a fine strategic partnership, killed by an attorney who probably understood the client requirements but was unwilling to offer flexible solutions to problem areas. That attorney had made what we considered business decisions on behalf of his client. By the way, we immediately found a willing replacement that had an attorney not quite so full of himself and quickly concluded a similar deal to the acceptance of all. And to this day, I caution my CEO's not to deal with that Fortune 500 firm because of the experience we had with its attorney. You never know how much far reaching an action can be, given the speed and extent of communication between CEO's today.

Accountants "plan-alyze". Bookkeepers count beans.

This is a distinction we need to repeat on occasion, especially for new CEO's looking to pay a low wage for advanced financial analysis, whether with an independent contractor or an employee. Accountants are trained, certified and usually quite experienced in financial analysis, both creating and reviewing data. Bookkeepers are often trained on the job although sometimes more formally, and handle the physical work of accounting for the transactions. To expect a bookkeeper to provide analytical planning is to ask for something they often cannot provide, except in a cursory way.

Why the discussion? Many early stage CEO's believe they can delegate design and creation of metrics, flash reports, analytical reports and more from their bookkeepers. And at some early stages, a bookkeeper is capable of preparing such information. It does not take long for a growing business and a knowledgeable CEO to quickly outgrow the lack of depth and sophistication such reporting usually offers, looking instead for deeper analytical tools.

On the other hand, many early stage CEO's are not trained and ready for such tools even if available. The lesson here is twofold. There is a benefit to using a good accountant to help devise critical reports for a corporation; and CEO's must quickly become financially savvy in the analysis of financial statements and metrics that measure the health of a business. To fail to have this skill is to reduce the corporation's capability to discover problems early and take advantage of growth opportunities.

Good tax planning is both legal and smart.

When do you cross the line between honesty and dishonesty in tax planning? Is it ethical to allocate income between periods to take advantage of tax breaks? Can expenses be put off until the next period to increase income, or accelerated into this period by prepayment to decrease net income? Where do you draw the line, assuming no intent to defraud?

First, corporations are usually on an accrual accounting basis, meaning that income and expenses are accounted for as earned, not when the cash is received. (You, on the other hand, account for your individual income on a cash-accounting bases, counting the cash not the date of your earning or accrued expense. The difference: If you earn pay due December 31st and it is paid January second, you pay income tax on those earnings in the following year. But the corporation that pays you accrues the expense and takes the deduction in the year in which the income was earned or expense actually incurred.)

It is perfectly legal to hold delivery of goods until after the start of the next period and take the income next year rather than this. It is a bit murky if you accelerate payment for incomplete services or even for products not yet received into this year to take the deduction from income early. In either an IRS audit or an accounting review or audit, the accelerated costs and payments will show as an accrual – a balance sheet item – that does not change income, just cash and an asset. In other words, for the usual accrual-based business, there are fewer ways to affect the outcome than for a cash-accounting individual. There are lots of caveats here and certainly if the issue is critical to you, an accountant (rarely a bookkeeper) should guide you to the action that is both legal and strategic.

Consultants are only as good as the as the advice you take.

At one time or another, most all businesses use consultants to fill the gaps in knowledge or to provide guidance for management. Consultants are good in that you can sample their work with short projects, change to other consultants quickly, and stop using them when a project is completed.

I have a partner in a consulting practice that specializes in the travel industry. Several years ago, we were hired by one of the largest companies in the industry (yet another Fortune 500) to perform a top-to-bottom audit of their processes across 27 facilities, and recommend measures to increase efficiency, increase income and of course, decrease costs while also increasing the quality of service. We were quite confident that our services would yield great, measurable results. The work continued for about eight weeks between the two of us as we visited the 27 locations and worked with employees in departments across all disciplines within each location and at central offices that performed services for all locations.

Finally, at the end of the project, we had identified nineteen specific issues, each of which would, if implemented, accomplish one or more of the goals outlined at the start of the project. The sum of the savings and increases in revenue were worth multi-millions annually, well worth the implementation of most or all of the recommendations.

On the final day of our assignment, I was responsible for the "reporting out" to the assembled twenty or so executives in the large conference room of this major corporation. I started my presentation, which had been carefully documented in handouts and PowerPoint, with this story…

"I want you to all imagine that it is tomorrow morning, looking back upon today's reporting of these past months of work by your consultants. Imagine that today I build for you a beautiful sand castle exactly at the water line of the ocean nearby. Tomorrow, we both will visit that beach and look at the water line, and find not a beautiful castle, but just smooth sand, just as it had been the day before building our beautiful sand castle. In other words, I would not be surprised if you accept our report today with enthusiasm, but then in the overwhelming rush of daily business, fail to implement few if any of these recommendations that you so enthusiastically received."

The story is true and the results were as I predicted. A few of the recommendations were implemented over time, one with great effect and even a national advertising campaign behind it (that you surely saw on TV). But most were just ignored. I imagine that our report sits today on someone's shelf, filed with others from past and from following months and years.

Unfortunately, it is human nature to enthusiastically ignore to act upon recommendations of third party consultants. There are many, many exceptions, but far more instances of this in the business world. Not all consultants give advice worth taking, of course. But when they do so, it is only as good as that which you implement.

What if you don't know what to ask?

Great executives and managers seem to intuitively know what they don't know. But it is not at all uncommon to not even know what questions to ask.

How do you avoid being sideswiped by the new product you never saw coming, or by the "black swan" event no-one ever thought of that might threaten your business?

Speaking with a roundtable group of fellow associates, most all of them CEOs, we addressed this question and spent an hour brainstorming how to protect against just such a lack of forward vision.

One CEO stated that she engages regularly in scenario planning with her executives, asking "what if" questions to explore the edges of the group's thinking about everything from disruptions of supply to changes in customer taste to acts of God such as floods or earthquake. The group agreed that this is an excellent process, engaging the entire team and members' experience to explore the unknown.

But what if no one in the group thinks to ask the pertinent question that leads to the most impactful unknown? What if that threat is outside of the experience of anyone in the room? What if no one knows what to ask?

Another CEO chimed in with an answer that made us all think. Most every technology advance has been predicted in works of fiction years before the fact, he stated. Why not look to fiction for clues? From devastating events like tsunamis to future user interfaces predicted in such films as *Star Trek* or *Minority Report*, there are liberating clues within the experiences of most of us. Think of *Flash Gordon* or *Dick Tracy*, characters from many decades ago with communication devices that have not only come to life but have been far surpassed in reality. Tom Cruise's virtual handling of graphics by hand movements came true only a few years later, even popularized as a game with Microsoft's Kinect system driven by body movement alone.

Our frame of reference must be as broad as possible when asking "what if" questions to protect our future. Read more science fiction if you are involved in technology. Read more disaster novels to expand your thinking to the very edge, even if only for a minute as you examine what and how to react to the unknowns that are sure to someday challenge us.

The "buggy whip" trap.

Surely you've heard the buggy whip analogy. A business making those necessary items ignored the signs of progress and found itself without a market. Perhaps that happened to sword smiths upon the invention of the rifle, and certainly to the makers of cassette tapes upon the dawn of the CD.

I found myself in the middle of such a slow-rolling change twice in my career. First, in the late 1960's (yes, I know, a long time ago), there were 31 phonograph record manufacturing plants in Southern California alone. By 1975, there were only two. That is sudden change, brought about by the fast acceptance of the cassette, which in turn gave way to the next technology, CDs, after a rather short lifecycle. Record plants were noisy, dirty places, using chemicals I can only imagine now rest somewhere in the ocean, to electroplate the "stampers" and press the records. Cassettes, in contrast, could be manufactured in small rooms with much less expensive equipment and no damage to the environment.

The second time I learned the buggy whip lesson was at the dawn of the personal computer age, and this time we guided our firm without a hitch from minicomputers to networked PCs, even growing the business as we gave up the lucrative $100,000 hardware sales in return for service fees to network our customers' systems, install our database, and migrate to customer-purchased desktop and servers.

Here it is, not so many years later, and the signs are more subtle yet, but the speed of obsolescence is much faster. Take for example, the public's quick acceptance of Facebook, Zinga, Mixi, and other social networking portals, leaving early leader MySpace wondering what happened to their comfortable lead and large fan base. With rapid sharing of information and recommendations, a fickle public can change its mass preferences seemingly in an instant.

How do you spot the buggy whip trap and differentiate it from a simple business cycle slump? The answer is simple, but somehow out of reach for most senior executives and entrepreneurs. Micro trends may seem to be a whisper, as mini-trends follow with leading adopters making a bit of noise. It is those leading adopters who take the chance on new technologies, new companies, new styles, and new idioms. That is why so many larger companies pay specialty marketing firms to find, court, and listen to those individuals who lead the pack in taste and action.

For those of us who don't have the resources to hire these expensive market trend-watching firms, there are more simple yet effective opportunities. Usually, technology and style trends begin with those aged between 15 and 23. And which of us doesn't have at least one close relative or child at or near these ages? Have you ever asked for an hour of such a relative's time to discuss what's "cool" or "coming" or "must have" in their lives?

It is human nature to protect one's investment of money, time and brand in an enterprise. That leads naturally to a resistance to change and inability to willingly move to replace your own product with something new that will kill its revenues.

But we all know that if we do not do it when offered the evidence of obsolescence, someone else will. So, are you investing in your own form of buggy whip product or service today?

Cash - is time - is cash.

Here is a simple economic truth. Fixed overhead continues to eat into your cash month after month. It doesn't differentiate facile, efficient businesses from slow, disorganized, quality-challenged ones.

If it takes eighteen months to get a new product out the door and into the market, and if a product's gross margin is ten dollars but the corporate overhead is a million a month, it will take the sale of 67,000 more units to break even than if it were to take only six months to market. If the total annual potential is 100,000 units, the slower cycle to market just cost the company two thirds of a year in the product's profits. With today's rapid obsolescence, that could be the entire life cycle of the product itself, lost because of being slow to market.

And profits from the sale of the product create cash for development of the next product. If the time to market is slowed by inefficient development, the risk of a competitive product overtaking yours increases dramatically.

So the truth of the statement is self-evident. Because fixed overhead burns cash, extended development cycles burn more cash, preventing earlier sale of product, to create even more cash. Efficiency in development pays off in less cost and earlier competitive products, often producing greater market share in the process.

Have you considered how to make your operation more efficient as an important way to increase cash flow? Most of us are quick to worry over cutting costs. Some of us worry over how to greatly increase revenues. Few of us worry over how to squeeze more efficiency out of the development cycle or from the organization itself.

That's your challenge for the day, week, and month.

Play Nice!

When you were a kid, surely at one time or another, Mom or someone reminded you to "play nice" when you got a bit rambunctious with your friends. I was reminded about this by Mark Wayman, a friend and reader, who applied this statement to his recruiting environment. He called out those people who focus upon executives who burned bridges with threats and lawsuits, instead of just picking up their toys and moving on after a bad business breakup.

Over the years, I have reminded departing employees in their exit interview that we should always, always both take the high ground and speak well of each other, since we never know when we will meet again under entirely different circumstances. And indeed, former employees (not necessarily disaffected or threatening in their departure) have shown up regularly as suppliers and customers in various companies in subsequent months and years.

There is no immediate gain in threats to an employee or by an employee. But there certainly is an immediate loss of respect and the start of a series of events that sometimes cannot be stopped. A threat of a lawsuit results in that person being immediately isolated and sometimes removed - if the employer believes there is enough evidence of misconduct or poor performance in the file to justify immediate termination.

Short of threats, bad-mouthing a former employer or employee is the worst possible behavior when considering the effect upon the corporate culture if the offender is the employer, and upon the person making the claim if by a former employee. The point is that no one wins in this kind of word war. And if it ever gets to a lawsuit, both parties lose a second time as the lawyers take control and costs escalate out of control.

Mom's advice is almost always right – for business as well as for personal relationships. Never strike out at anyone before first cooling off and thinking about the relative worth of the effort against the long term gain or loss. The resulting effort will be surely muted and couched in a way that you'll avoid retribution.

Hold on to some "sticky" cash.

It is tempting to use available cash in good times to build the business and in challenging times to pay the bills and even to outdo competitors in marketing efforts. Those are both good strategies. But there is a tactic that we need to remember that just might save the business.

Once a business has achieved breakeven and beyond, it should build a cash reserve equal to at least two months' worth of fixed overhead to protect against unexpected internal or external emergencies, and to allow for a relatively restful slumber at night for those who must worry about cash balances.

Good businesses keep that "sticky" cash in a money market account, not because of its earnings potential, which is usually so small as to be inconsequential, but because it is visible and requires effort to invade the balance.

Seasonal businesses are more challenged, and sticky cash has more of a meaning, since it must see the enterprise through the low seasons. For these types of businesses, short term bank loans are an ideal way to augment cash flow and finance receivables during high season, always assuming that the loans will be paid off in full from seasonal receipts.

Remember the term. Isolate the reserves. Maintain the discipline as soon as able.

Update your banker in good times and bad.

You've heard the old one – that a banker always seems willing to offer a loan when you don't need it. For small businesses, there is such truth in that statement that you can trust the story to be based in reality from experience.

There are great exceptions for growing businesses and for businesses that have a track record with a banker. Working capital loans and lines of credit are needed for growth and during times of business stress. If a business were operating above breakeven and revenues and expenses steady, profits would flow to either the shareholders' pockets or to working capital and taxes. Each cycle gives the CEO a chance to use those profits to some positive advantage, including increasing the marketing budget, paying down loans, building working capital, increasing "sticky cash" balances or paying shareholders.

But if a good business finds itself in a bad downturn, there may be a need that did not exist before for temporary cash, even as management reacts and moves to trim fixed overhead.

Approaching a banker during such times tests relationships. If there was no previous relationship, few bankers would rely upon anything but a personal guarantee backed by hard assets before considering a loan. But for those wise executives who included their bankers in occasional update calls, press releases, invitations to company events and an occasional personal visit, the strength of the relationship will often show its benefits during times when lending rules of the bank are near the "can't do it" point.

For those with existing bank loans, that constant attention is more than just important. As loan covenants become closer to being violated or after such an event, bankers have some latitude in deciding how to handle their accounts. Upon discovery without prior notice or updates, bankers sometimes turn the company over to the bank's workout group – a place you never want to visit. In the gray area where covenants are broken but barely, covenants can be waived for a period of time as companies rectify the problems, all based upon the quality of the relationship between banker and client.

It is during those challenging times that it is most difficult to tell the story to your banker, but just then the most important of times.

Short term leases early on. Move as you grow.

Avoid long-term commitments.

It is statistically true that at least half of the young companies funded by angel or venture investors will not survive three years from funding to demise. The greatest burden of either a growing company or one needing to retract and reduce expenses is the office lease. Although payroll is almost always the greatest cost, companies have flexibility as to how to handle both rapid growth and rapid decline in the personnel arena.

The most difficult thing to deal with in either rapid growth or retrenchment is the office lease. A five year lease may be cheaper than a three year lease, and may provide for more free rent and tenant improvements. Those benefits pale in comparison to the high cost in retaining or buying out a longer term lease.

From personal experience with many companies in my portfolio and from many board experiences over the years, young companies are unpredictably unstable in their facilities requirements. Flexibility is worth a few percentage points of fixed cost when companies are in high growth mode or are at early stages of proof of market.

It is a hassle to move, requiring time and planning. It is much worse to worry over paying for two leases each month and tying up two large deposits. Then there is the dread of "The tyranny of the new office" to worry about. But that is a story for the next insight...

Pay for frequent moves over risky long leases.

One of the most obvious observations I make with growing company CEO's is that planning for a new office is done with an optimistic view of the future, incorporating planned space that compromises only slightly the measured needs for the next three or more years as outlined in the financial forecast.

The result, signing a lease for space enough to handle the growth called for in the plan, is a predictable group behavior I've come to label *"The tyranny of the new office."* The company plans a move to a new facility with plenty of space that is probably built out but not planned for use until the company grows to the next stage of need. Employees move into their new cubicles and offices, spread out far more than in the previous facility. The excitement and noise of working in too-close proximity to cohorts suddenly becomes an unexpected near silence, as everyone notices that they do not have to raise their voices any more to be heard above the din of noise.

The exciting sounds of an office filled to capacity functioning in a growth environment are exhilarating to most that have experienced it. The distractions are dealt with using iPods and earphones, concentration and tolerance; but they are dealt with by all. The change to a near silent environment is so startling that, many times, employees express a bit of resentment or even depression, masked by the common statement that "it is so much easier to get work done without the noise." It is the excitement of activity that generates more and better output for most, not the isolation of silence.

But back to "the tyranny of the new office." Two predictable outcomes almost always follow a move into an office much larger than today's needs. First, you'll find subtle moves by employees into the unused, reserved space. After all, it is there and unneeded for now. Why not make use of the space until needed? And second, management sees the open space and often finds it easier to justify acceleration of one or more new hires since the facility is available and infrastructure complete. Unconsciously longing for a bit more of the excitement from the noise of the previous office, managers often make subtle unrecognized moves to fill the void with new hires earlier than plan. That's why the label, "tyranny" even if the word seems out of context.

If and when asked, I always recommend more frequent moves as opposed to longer term leases. It seems from experience that both the company and the employees gain from such staggered moves.

Refresh your enthusiasm for the job.

So you've been at this for years through thick and thin, great days and days in which you've had better times. Much of your job has become routine. But it feels good to see your "baby" grow and others buy into your vision.

It is human nature for you and every entrepreneur to fall into a routine of taking care of day to day issues, meetings, communicating with customers and shareholders. But you remember the thrilling days when everything was newer, each decision an event, each milestone something to be celebrated. If you think about it, you also remember that you spent much more of your time on strategic issues and thinking about the business and its growth, as opposed to thinking within the business about its process issues.

Your value as a CEO or executive is inherent in creating the vision, providing the drive, and forcing focus upon successful implementation of the vision that you bring to the enterprise. It is where the fun is.

So, how do you regain that enthusiasm for what is best for you and for the company? There are a number of things you can and should do, and soon.

Take a day – a full day – off to walk, sit, and think of where you want this company and your role in it to be in the future. Don't let interruptions from emails, phone calls and people at the door interfere with this focused effort.

Then call a strategic planning session, off site, for you, your board, your advisors, and direct reports. If needed, hire a facilitator. And provide for someone to take notes. Lay out your vision to those present as a starting point. Ask for comments, challenges, and additions. Then spend the rest of the day developing strategies and tactics to get you there. Finish the process by refining the resulting document, passing it through the same group for comments. Then call an all-company meeting to focus everyone on the vision, goal, strategies and tactics. Stand back and watch for the reaction. Most everyone wants direction and to buy into a vision that makes their jobs have meaning.

Starting the very next day, begin monitoring progress toward the goal or goals, raising your job to one of strategic implementation and guidance, not of day-to-day process.

Your value will increase in the minds of your board, and you will feel much more enthusiastic about your contributions to the success of your enterprise.

It's your move.

Disaster Recovery and other happy subjects.

Have you ever lost all of your data on your smartphone, laptop, or desktop PC? If not, it is probably only a matter of time until you do. Those of us who have experienced this heart-stopping event now regularly back up our data and many of us create images of our entire hard drives often, ready this time to address an effective recovery.

But what about the shock of a fire, a major natural disaster, or even the loss of an important company top executive? Are you or your board prepared to immediately jump into a pre-planned recovery? From experience on more than forty boards over the years, I can state that few have even considered the possibilities. All of us have a phone listing of our employees and associates. But very few have a phone tree for simultaneous contact of larger numbers of people to marshal a recovery from any type of disaster.

Boards of directors for companies of all sizes should have a person or better yet a committee dedicated to considering the preparations for disaster recovery. Often, we consolidate this task into the audit committee of a board; and often we expand the subject to 'risk management' which includes examination of all forms of risk, from insurance coverage to OSHA compliance and more.

When a company is very small and the company's assets reasonably replaceable with existing or easily borrowed funds, the event is less likely to threaten the existence of the organization. As a company grows in size and complexity, more stakeholders depend upon the wisdom of the CEO and the board to think in advance of these unpleasant things, and to attempt to insulate the company's dependents from a disaster.

How about yourself? Have you been open in sharing your knowledge and talent with a backup, or even a potential successor? It is prudent and certainly a sign that you take this responsibility personally as a leader among your peers and subordinates.

I have three unfortunate examples in my past of founder-CEOs dying suddenly at their prime. The shock to each organization was a threat to the very core in all three instances. Yet as we will discuss in detail in a future insight, in one, the board stepped in immediately to reassure the stakeholders, elect a new CEO from within the board, and reach out to the community with a plan for succession that allowed the business to continue with minimal interruption. In another, the creditors threatened to close the company, and the board was completely unprepared to respond. The contrast was quite a lesson to me – one that I would never want to repeat as a board member or senior manager.

What if? How about dedicating at least a half hour of your next executive or board meeting to the subject, and creating a checklist and assignments for covering at least the greatest three risks identified? It is yet another sign of your growth and growing wisdom as a leader.

Safety first. Profits follow.

Much of work place safety is common sense. But there is a natural tension between economy of operation and provision for safety for employees, and the resulting risk to the enterprise must be carefully weighed.

Good boards of directors have a committee of the board to deal with "audit" issues, which should include analysis and recommendations to management about workplace safety as a part of a broader issue of risk management. After all, the board and management together are responsible for keeping the company alive, protecting the corporate asset on behalf of all stakeholders - including shareholders, employees, and customers.

Especially in a manufacturing environment, there are laws created by those who have experienced the result of accidents by others that impose upon all companies the hard-earned lessons from the past. Many of us groan when reading or hearing of these detailed, burdensome rules and laws. Yet workplace accidents are harmful to health and safety for all, to morale, and they ultimately cause financial hardships upon the company, whether in the form of lost productivity, increased insurance cost, or debilitating lawsuits that inevitably follow.

No company, even the smallest, is immune to safety issues. In this computer keyboard-driven office world, programmers, accounting and office personnel, and many others are exposed to carpel tunnel, back, and leg and neck problems, just by sitting in place. The risk of injury, worker compensation insurance claim, lost productivity, and lawsuit are only slightly less in the office than on the factory floor.

And how do you protect your employees who travel when on the road? Are you and they aware of the procedures for informing insurance companies, their managers and others in the event of an accident while on the road? How do you and they respond when out of the country? To whom do they turn when in unsafe environments, let alone after an accident, when isolated from their local infrastructure?

None of us likes to think of these issues which detract from the focus upon growth and customer service. But these very issues can derail the best of organizations at the worst of times. At the very least, management and its board should discuss the exposures to safety risks and how they might be mitigated in advance.

Corporate whistle-blowers fulfill a function.

Assuming first that a corporate whistle-blower is not tooting about you individually, such a class of people have been granted protections under the law and serve a function that needs to be acknowledged.

First, the assumption is that such a person is not making his or her gesture for personal profit, but to give proper notice that there is something illegal going on within the company that the person cannot accept and must tell someone about. Note that I use the word "illegal" to differentiate the tell-tale from the legitimate whistle-blower. A tell-tale almost always has a motive based upon political or personal gain, with the exception of when there is a perception or the reality of any form of sexual interference or bullying being reported. That's a subject for a separate discussion, and there are civil penalties as recourse for such proven behavior.

Whistle-blowers, on the other hand, if not motivated by a personal reward, are often brave beyond need, risking job and reputation to call attention to an illegal act or acts. If the person comes to you with evidence of such acts, you must act immediately to address the issue, often including reporting the incident to the authorities along with the whistle-blower. That's particularly tough if the consequence is going to be severe against the company itself. But, if we have learned anything at all from the last several decades of such incidents reported from within highly visible companies, covering up the problem results in amplifying it beyond anyone's wildest imagination. Quickly dealing with it and the consequences always is the lesser of numerous alternatives.

And of course, the whistle-blower is protected by law and cannot be punished in any way for the deed of reporting a wrongdoing that breaks the law, *whether later proved true or false*.

Some agencies offer cash rewards for whistle-blowers that are in proportion to the amount recaptured by a taxing authority or penalties assessed. Such rewards blur the heroic act into one where personal gain can easily be assumed to be more of a motive for a good deed than brave action. And there are raging arguments from company offices to the halls of Congress about whether a whistle-blower should or must first approach senior management within the company before reporting to authorities. But, no matter what the outcome or how high the reward, that does not change the protection the whistle-blower has under the law.

Insurance is always too expensive until needed.

This insight seems obvious to most anyone. But it is a fact that business insurance is one of the more poorly managed mitigations of risk in small and some medium sized corporations, often because of failure to assign the responsibility to an individual or department, and sometimes just from the willingness to bet against the event and save cash.

Business package policies are inexpensive and rather comprehensive tools that should be contracted by all companies with any assets to measure and protect. A typical beginning package for a small company costs about $4 thousand a year, and covers a number of forms of liability both premises and product as well as employee use of self-owned cars for work, theft, employee dishonesty and more. There is usually a small amount of business interruption insurance in the standard package, and more protection can be added at a cost. Reading the list of protections is both impressive and frightening, since most of us never think of such risks, and it is overwhelming to have them pointed out in one reading. Conversely, the list of excluded protections is equally frightening for the same reason. We do not think of these unless someone points them out.

I believe my former software firm was responsible for one such exclusion that used to be a standard part of such policies. (Sorry about that.) With almost 250 employees, 26 of whom were application programmers, it was important to back up the work of these programmers each night, and an employee was tasked with just this each evening after midnight. Each night's backup would be carefully marked and the rotated between offsite and on-site locations in a series of steps so that backups of a day, two days, a week and a month were all available both on site and off site. Did I fail to mention that for more than a year we never tested whether the backups actually contained good data? It seems that a change in the operating system on the server we used for development was made that changed the way backups were cued, and our backup person was unaware of the procedural change needed to accommodate this. Came the inevitable day of the massive head crash, I quickly heard of the problem and the fact that all 26 programmers were standing by waiting for the backup to be restored, expecting to lose the partial day's work.

And the first backup from the night before was blank. As was each subsequent backup, on-site and offsite. It took weeks for the team to assemble code from various sources such as customer sites, beta test locations and demo machines. Then it took another several weeks for the programmers to come back up to speed rewriting patches and programs in a frustrating recreation of weeks and more worth of previous work.

I tasked our accounting department with collecting and calculating the costs of the labor lost, which was the only real claim for business interruption to be made as customers were unaffected by the problem. The cost came to well over $100 thousand, and a claim was filed with the business package insurer. After a short negotiation and quick audit, the insurance company paid $108 thousand to settle the claim. In the following year's renewal policy, I noticed a new page in the exclusions section, excluding for the first time data losses from failed backups, no matter what the cause or where the fault. As I recall, the year was 1987. Either we were the first to make a significant claim under this previously covered portion of the policy or one of several that did so in that year. Either way, you have me to blame for one more of those exclusion pages that overwhelm such policies today.

A worker compensation policy is not optional.

This is one that early stage CEO's are almost universally unaware of. Most every state requires that any company with employees be covered by a policy of insurance against claims by workers for injury on the job, or worker compensation insurance. Many states has privately owned but state-overseen state insurance funds for this purpose, and of course a number of private companies offer such insurance alone or along with business package policies.

In this increasingly litigious employment environment, it is mandatory for a company of any size to maintain worker comprehensive insurance. I have experienced incidents of claims that seemed quite minor on the surface where the employee was able to claim and receive large payments, sometimes over extended periods, for carpal tunnel injuries, slips and falls, neck injuries and more. Claims worth half a million or more are not uncommon. It may seem like an employee's lottery win to management, but the fact of the insurance award is real. In most states, the CEO and other executive owners of the corporation may be exempted from the policy and the costs reduced accordingly. Also, each employee is classified according to job performed, with some drawing very high premiums relative to others. With your agent's help, you should be very careful to place employees in the proper but most advantageous class for the sake of the policy.

Also, you will find all insurers asking for an estimate of gross payroll costs in advance of each policy year. At the conclusion of each year, before renewal, the insurance company will perform an audit of your payroll and bill the company for underestimated amounts, or credit the company for overestimation. These audits are often merely by telephone to your bookkeeper for small companies, rising to physical audits of submitted documents or in person for larger enterprises. Treat such policies seriously. For a reasonable cost, they protect against the strangest and saddest of employee-based corporate liabilities.

Employee first, company last, states the law.

Almost all laws dealing with employment are designed to protect the employee, not the company. Minimum wage laws, workplace safety, independent contractor tests, minimum hours required for benefits, worker compensation insurance requirements and more are examples of such laws. Notice that every poster that is required to be displayed in a company public area (usually the lunch room) is posted for the benefit of the employee to inform him or her of rights granted by law. To most entrepreneurs, this often leads to an event whose resolution by a governmental agency or even a court seems unfair and illogical. Issues that seem clearly based upon ineptitude morph into age or gender-related epic battles that most always end poorly.

So my advice is simple. Recognize the realities of the times, and do all possible to protect the company by documenting behavioral or skill related problems to the employee file. Hold regular reviews for all your employees right to the top. (The chairman reviews the CEO, and if there is no separate chairperson, then the CEO should ask an outside board member to do so.) Encourage reviewers to be accurate, not just polite, in documenting areas of concern.

This is not to counter the advice of insight number 27, "Fire fast, not last", since every CEO should shoot for "A" class employees and not tolerate underperformers over time.

The 18 month rule.

It can take 18 months from initial concern about a critical employee to getting a replacement up to speed.

This insight is not mine, although I have experienced it several times with key employees since becoming sensitive to the concept. An old friend, Dick Tanaka, gets credit for this one. He observed that the process we follow to be humane in our handling of underperforming employees, manage the risk of future lawsuit, finally then move to separate the employee, define the open position, recruit the candidate, train the new hire and count the new hire as up to speed in the job can take all of eighteen months.

That is a shock in so many ways. First, the costs for underperformance are both tangible and intangible, with lost revenues, lost opportunities, lost savings and loss of productivity from low employee morale difficult to estimate. There are those in the recruiting industry that have attempted to do so, and depending upon the size of the company and the position replaced, seeming to settle upon astronomical lost costs that overwhelm most of our ability to understand. All of us will admit that, looking back at a failed employee hire, the costs were well beyond the payroll cost for the individual.

Perhaps this is a good time to speak about senior managers that are well-entrenched in the organization but are underperformers because the organization has passed their ability or span of control. We will explore this in detail in a future insight, but it is important to note the trauma of separating an old friend or close associate, or even a family member. There are few good rules for conduct in these instances, other than honesty in pointing out the problems, and doing everything possible to preserve the individual's dignity.

Early in the rapid growth phase of my computer software company, I hired an excellent, IBM-trained vice president of sales to further growth and begin our international expansion. He did so with gusto, and for several years was directly responsible for our growth into a total of 29 countries, including establishment of six foreign subsidiaries. Annual growth in revenues was between 50% and 100%, amazing and exhilarating. But he had a habit of bellowing out at underperformers, bullying others to get his way, and doing so in ways that rubbed all other managers the wrong way as he dominated meetings, and made it difficult for others to contribute. Surely a result more of his urban New York upbringing, I put up with these character traits as the cost for his amazing performance. And you might guess that, as his superior, I did not experience any of the threats to my job or dignity that apparently all others did.

I received a call one day from one of my country managers, stating that he and all of my senior managers would be at a meeting room in a nearby hotel the next evening at 7.00 PM, and that the vice president of sales, presently in the air traveling to the very country where the manager was to meet him, was not to be present. I was shocked and disoriented, a CEO with no idea of the urgency of the situation that was developing, since there had been no warning. Fourteen people, including the country managers and all the vice presidents, were to be there. I immediately called an industrial psychologist I knew, asking him to be at my side during the meeting to listen and interpret the mood of the meeting. (I have an industrial psychology educational background, but could not count upon myself to be completely objective here, of course.)

We walked into the meeting at the appointed time. Apparently the meeting had been going for some hours. Everyone but the sales VP was present as anticipated. As the psychologist and I listened to one after another of these, my most senior talent minus one, describe the assaults to their very souls, the affronts to their self-respect, the hobbling of their ability to perform, I was overwhelmed. There had been comments from some of these individuals in the past, but never voiced as an orchestra, and never with evidence so overwhelming and irrefutable. As the presentations of each concluded, my senior-most VP stood and stated calmly that if I would not remove the affronting individual, each and every one of the people present had agreed to resign. Now that's an act of desperation or defiance rare, perhaps unique.

I asked for a few minutes to confer with my associate. You might guess that it took less than that. As we returned to the room, I turned to the psychologist, the only third party in the room, and asked him to give the group his candid response to what he had heard. As I recall, he stated quite clearly that in many instances he is hired to repair relationships at senior levels in companies with such problems, paying special attention to coaching and training the offender, sensitizing him or her to the traits probably not noticed in self. But, he stated, as I recall, "This one is for the books." He had no advice other than to just do it and now. Of course, I had come to the same conclusion, even though at least in the short term, sales growth would suffer.

The rest of this story, if I took the time to tell it, would deal with the humanity of this next step, and retention of the dignity of a superior performer in all ways but one in his management abilities and in dealing with contemporaries and subordinates. I recalled him immediately back to corporate headquarters, and fired him after discussing the reasons with care, negotiating a reasonable separation package. The culture of the company thrived, and I could feel a collective sigh of relief from people even far below the level of senior management. And, although we have little contact after all these years, I have remained friends with this superior performer to this day. He understood, acknowledged the personality trait that failed him as one that had haunted him in his past, and became part of the solution once he and I had all of the facts on the table. It is a story that is extreme, relies upon one fatal character trait, but in other ways probably could match one or more of your own stories to tell or someday to experience.

Never run out of money.

Money in the bank is like oil in the car.

This is such an obvious observation that you should think that it does not rise to the level of an "insight". Yet, there is sage advice behind this statement that I could not ignore placing it right in the middle of these insights. As an executive, you have many ways you are pulled every day, both tactical and strategic. But when money is the issue, your time, energy and focus are drained from other important areas of the business.

Running out of money is not always synonymous with "going broke". Many great businesses in their growth periods find themselves stretched for cash. If fixed expenses, especially payroll, are paid out before cash is received from services or shipments, the company is financing its growth with ever-increasing working capital needs. Without remaining availability from a bank line, many businesses are stretched to the limit just when they seem to be doing better than ever. This is one interpretation of *"It takes money to make money"*, although that statement was probably created to describe new investment opportunities.

Speaking of which, those companies with cash in the bank and cash available are the ones to scoop up the bargains, from suppliers and in acquisitions especially during tough times.

But the most important lesson to learn is that cash is the great lubricant for businesses. Without at least a month's working capital needs on hand in the form of cash, receivables that will be cash, or an untapped credit line as a fallback, the CEO should worry over cash flow issues on a daily basis. Any disruption to the tedium of daily activity from weather, disaster, revenues slowdown or product problems will stress the company infrastructure if there is not a cushion to use during such times. Stress of this type always forces senior management to lose focus upon strategic issues and drop into day-to-day tactical mode.

I find it a great thrill to consult to companies and their senior management when they have plenty of "firepower" (extra cash beyond needs) for acquisitions and strategic initiatives. It seems that the first subject that comes up in such assignments is the health of the competition. Such bargains; so little time.

Running out of cash denigrates the very value of a business, reducing greatly any bargaining power with suppliers or acquirers. A company that otherwise might be valued at twice book value, 1x revenues, or 10 times earnings will be valued at a lower amount by potential acquirers knowing that the company shareholders are in a tough position and management hungry for leverage and a little more sleep at night.

Never run out of money, even at the expense of slowing growth for a time. A fast-growing but undercapitalized company is not highly valued in an acquisition. For early stage businesses worrying over dilution when faced with an offer of more money than they need, the professional advice is most often to take the money and suffer the dilution because the money may not be available if needed later.

Cash is such a powerful inhibitor or driver of growth that management of the corporate cash is as important as strategic vision, and perhaps over time a good indication of the success of that vision to drive profits.

When cash is tight, slow its flight.

We have discussed *why* never to run out of cash. This insight delves into *how* never to run out of cash. There are four basic ways to increase the cash position of a company: inject cash through borrowing or investment, decrease spending or payments on debt, increase efficiency of operations, and increase revenues or advance payments from customers.

Even before examining the tactics of cash flow management, we've got to acknowledge that you never, ever should slip on payment of payroll taxes. The temptation to do so in tight times is tremendous, but the liability for such taxes are personal to senior management as individuals and cannot be waived or negotiated away. I advise all of my companies to use an impressed payroll service, one that takes the taxes from your bank account along with the net payrolls each period. I have a story about this for later in this insight. A close second for the same reasons are sales taxes and income taxes. Both of these take a bit longer for the appropriate authority to move to freeze accounts because the processes of doing so are more involved. But all forms of tax must be paid to avoid catastrophe, if not merely avoid 25% penalties.

Let's examine decrease in spending first. There are several classes of obligations and several types of providers within each. Assuming that the company is not already on the "cash only" list from materials suppliers requiring payment to those just to keep the business flowing, then when cash is tight, payments to ongoing providers of necessary services or products must rise near the top of the list. If there are several alternative suppliers of the same service that regularly deal with the company, then you have more power in lengthening payments to one. Calling vendors when payment is due but missed is always appropriate and will buy the company time and good will. But promises made must be kept, even if the amounts of payment are small. Some people advise that a company make small payments of any size to most all vendors, stating that these will keep the wolf from the door during tough times. I agree, but spreading the cash prevents making significant payments to those vendors needed most for continuing operations, and the balance is worth careful consideration.

In general, next in line are those that charge stiff penalties for late payment, including landlords and credit card companies. Often last are the lawyers and accountants who protect you and help you to plan your recovery, only because they above all others are vested with you in your recovery and success.

Accelerating revenues comes next. Close supervision of delinquent receivables is time-consuming but absolutely necessary. There are statistics that show clearly that the likelihood of payment drops quickly as receivables age beyond terms. And I've seen many company receivables clerks do a stunning job of collecting right on time by calling a few days ahead of time to check on the progress of a pending payment.

Thirty years ago, I stretched to buy a new home for my family that was above my ability to borrow at the time, but a bargain in a fast-rising market. My solution, aside from a first and second mortgage, was to call a number of my best customer CEO's, explain the problem-opportunity and ask for early payment of receivables. I promised each and later delivered a boatload of extra value for that evidence of good faith. As I recall, every one of the CEO's agreed to advance payments, and I did reward them with extra services. What may have seemed as a sign of weakness turned into a long term celebration of mutual trust and respect among peers.

Many companies have recurring revenues, often billed in advance, for maintenance or other services. Merely sending out the invoices for each period's pre-billing up to a month in advance of the start of the period will accelerate cash flow considerably. Many companies ask for deposits before performing services. Increasing the percentage of a contract as deposit is often unquestioned by small to mid-sized customers. Large corporations, those probably most able to pay such deposits, are usually the first to push back, often quoting "policy", whatever that is, as the authority preventing compliance with such a request.

I promised a story about payroll taxes, and it is not a good one, despite the best of intentions. One of my companies where I serve as chairman used a payroll service company that impressed payroll taxes along with payroll employee direct deposits and remitted those taxes directly to the authorities. Well, almost. One quarter, the company just did not receive its copies of the quarterly reports. I had wisely suspected this payroll company already and had the company switch to QuickBooks Payroll at the start of the new quarter. It turns out that the two founders of the small payroll services company absconded with (stole) all of the taxes from all of their payroll clients from mid-May through end of June that year. Since no tax authority notified any clients during those weeks no-one was aware that the money was gone and forms never filed. Millions were stolen. It is now years later, and our company as well as others have double-paid all the taxing authorities those missing taxes, including interest, but with penalties waived. The two founders are in Federal prison and about five percent of the missing funds were recovered by the Justice Department and returned to the companies. So it seems that even conservative cash tactics such as using an impressed service for payroll can lead to disaster. Who knew?

Provide for succession well in advance of need.

When we are young and early in our business lives, we feel infallible to the degree that we do not think of what might happen if we die while in office or decide to leave the company for any reason. Such thoughts just do not occur to most of us until the business is substantially far enough along in its growth to have multiple layers of management and enough employees and stakeholders that there is a board of directors and calls for key man insurance and succession planning.

Yet, I have written about three instances where I personally observed relatively young CEOs die while in their prime and while in office. In each case, from five to hundreds of employees depended upon the continuation of the business and looked to the board of directors for immediate assurance that a plan was in place. And in the three cases, there was none. However, in each case there was a board of directors, and each board moved to protect the corporation quickly as people absorbed the shock of loss. The outcomes were quite different with one board fending off immediate threats of lawsuit by creditors, another coaching a key employee into the CEO job, and the third electing a board member with experience to step in as CEO.

This is one sticky conversation for most young executives. Have you thought of who might succeed you if you are incapacitated or worse? Have you documented your position so a successor would know not only what you do but enough of how it is done to perform necessary functions early on? It is rare when either is in place, yet experience has proved that none of us is infallible and planning for succession is a protection for those left behind.

About the author...

Dave Berkus has a proven track record in operations, venture investing and corporate board service, both public and private. As an entrepreneur, he has formed, managed and sold successful businesses in the entertainment and software arenas. As a private equity investor, he has obtained healthy returns from liquidity events in over a dozen investments in early-stage ventures. As a corporate mentor and director, he was named *"Director of the Year"* for his directorship efforts with over 40 companies in the past decade.

Dave was the founder of ***Computerized Lodging Systems Inc.***, *(CLS),* which he guided as founder and CEO for over a decade that included two consecutive years on the *Inc.500* list of America's fastest growing companies, expansion to six foreign subsidiaries and twenty-nine foreign distributors, while capturing 16% of the world market for his enterprise products. Known as a hospitality industry visionary with many "firsts" to his credit and for his accomplishments in advancing technology in the hospitality industry, in 1998 he was inducted into the ***Hospitality (HFTP) "International Hall of Fame,"*** one of only thirty so honored worldwide over the years.

He has made over 100 investments in early stage ventures, for which he has an IRR of 97%, which includes capital contributions to his two funds (***Berkus Technology Ventures, LLC*** and ***Kodiak Ventures, L.P.***, for which he is the managing partner). He is also Chairman Emeritus of the Tech Coast Angels, one of the largest angel networks in the United States.

In recognition for adding significant shareholder value for emerging technology companies over the past decade, he was named ***"Director of the Year-Early Stage Businesses"*** by the *Forum for Corporate Directors* of Orange County, California and ***"Technology Leader of the Year"*** by the Los Angeles County Board of Supervisors. Dave currently sits on ten corporate boards and four non-profit boards.

Dave is also a senior partner in the twenty year old consulting firm of *Hospitality Automation Consultants, LTD (HACL)*, and lends his considerable visionary and strategic talents to worldwide hospitality chains and groups. He is the partner responsible for business process reorganization, strategic planning, software development and wide-area network infrastructure, and enterprise management systems.

A graduate of Occidental College, Dave currently serves as a Trustee of the College. Aside from this book, he is author of fourteen other books, twelve in the ***BERKONOMICS*** series, ***"Extending the Runway"*** originally published by Aspatore Press (and now by the BERKUS Press), and co-author of ***"Better than Money!"*** All are books for emerging growth technology company executives. Dave serves as Board Member of the San Gabriel Valley Council of ***Boy Scouts of America***, former Board Member of the ***Forum for Corporate Directors***, and is Chairman of the Advisory Board of the technology arm of the ***ABL Organization***, a networking organization of CEOs in high tech businesses.

He is often engaged as keynote speaker for events worldwide, speaking on trends in technology and of legal and practical issues of governance for emerging company corporate boards. He tells stories of entrepreneurs who have wildly succeeded or failed, deriving lessons from each for his audience. His TEDx talk, *"Smile at success; Laugh at failure,"* is available on YouTube as are other of segments of his keynotes. His televised *"Berkus Report"* segment of *Eye on Business*, can be found on Time Warner cable and other cable channels nationwide.

To contact Mr. Berkus for speaking engagements or workshops, email dberkus@berkus.com , or phone (626)355-5375. Dave's books are available for purchase from the above website, or the same source from which this book was purchased.

Subscribe to the free weekly email or blog, www.Berkonomics.com, containing much of the information from Dave's books with lots of comments from readers with their own stories to tell.

Follow Dave on Twitter (@daveberkus) and Facebook (Dave.Berkus).

Other books by Dave Berkus available directly from *www.berkus.com* or from your favorite bookseller or online store:

EXTENDING THE RUNWAY
Aspatore Press / Thompson West Publications

The five tools board members and executives can use to help their companies succeed. How boards and CEOs should relate to each other for growing the enterprise. Fifty-eight critical questions boards and management should consider in order to assure their mutual alignment.

BASIC BERKONOMICS
Hard cover, soft cover and eBook editions

Volume one of this series. Over one hundred critical insights for entrepreneurs, CEOs and board members covering the life of the company from ignition through liquidity event. Written with basic explanations for terms and methods, as well as insights into planning and measurement for success with small business startups.

BERKONOMICS
Hard cover, soft cover and eBook editions

Volume two of this series. One hundred and one critical insights for entrepreneurs, CEOs and board members covering the life of the company from ignition through liquidity event. Dave tells over fifty stories to illustrate his insights, culled from his experience as entrepreneur and service on over forty corporate and ten non-profit boards.

BERKONOMICS WORKBOOK

Companion to BERKONOMICS, this very personal journal contains 101 exercises for the CEO or manager that make each of the insights contained in BERKONOMICS come to life in the form of provocative and actionable questions to be answered right on the pages of the workbook. Once completed, this workbook becomes the manager's personal blueprint for business growth.

ADVANCED BERKONOMICS

Hard cover, soft cover and eBook editions

Volume two of this series. One hundred and one critical insights for entrepreneurs, CEOs and board members covering the life of the company from ignition through liquidity event. More advanced insights into planning and measurement for success with small business startups.

SMALL BUSINESS SUCCESS SERIES

A Series of eight short and inexpensive books or eBooks

Take all the great material in the BERKONOMICS series and slice it by subject, and you'll have these eight inexpensive, short books about issues that you and your management team needs to focus upon today. Ideal for giving to your entire management group for group discussions and business planning sessions.

BOOKS and eBOOKS IN THIS SERIES:

1. *Starting up!*
2. *Raising Money*
3. *Positioning for Success*
4. *Managing your Workforce*
5. *Protecting your Business*
6. *Growing your Business*
7. *Building Great Boards*
8. *Cashing Out!*

www.ingramcontent.com/pod-product-compliance
Lightning Source LLC
Chambersburg PA
CBHW021920170526
45157CB00005B/2118
9781105040726